Fran Brill and J. Smith-Cameron in a scene from the Circle Repertory production of "Desdemona, a play about a handkerchief." Set design by Derek McLane.

DESDEMONA

a play about a handkerchief

BY PAULA VOGEL

★

DRAMATISTS
PLAY SERVICE
INC.

DESDEMONA
Copyright © 1994, Paula Vogal

All Rights Reserved

SPECIAL NOTE

SPECIAL NOTE ON SONGS AND RECORDINGS

DESDEMONA, a play about a handkerchief, was produced by Circle Repertory Company (Tanya Berezin, Artistic Director; Abigail Evans, Managing Director), in New York City, in November, 1993. It was directed by Gloria Muzio; the set design was by Derek McLane; the costume design was by Jess Goldstein; the lighting design was by Michael Lincoln; the fight direction was by Rick Sordelet; the original music and sound design were by Randy Freed and the production stage manager was Fred Reinglas. The cast was as follows:

EMILIA	Fran Brill
DESDEMONA	J. Smith-Cameron
BIANCA	Cherry Jones

DESDEMONA, a play about a handkerchief, was originally produced in association with Circle Repertory Company by Bay Street Theatre Festival (Sybil Christopher and Emma Walton, co-Artistic Producers; Stephen Hamilton, Executive Producer), in Sag Harbor, New York, on July 23, 1993. It was directed by Gloria Muzio; the set design was by Derek McLane; the costume design was by Jess Goldstein; the lighting design was by Michael Lincoln; the original music and sound design were by Randy Freed and the production stage manager was Christopher Wigle. The cast was as follows:

EMILIA	Fran Brill
DESDEMONA	J. Smith-Cameron
BIANCA	Cherry Jones

3

CHARACTERS

DESDEMONA — Upper-class. Very.
EMILIA — Broad Irish Brogue.
BIANCA — Stage Cockney.

PLACE

A back room of the palace on Cyprus.

TIME

Ages ago.

The prologue takes place one week before Desdemona's last day on Cyprus.

NOTE TO DIRECTOR

DESDEMONA was written in thirty cinematic "takes"; the director is encouraged to create different pictures to simulate the process of filming: change invisible camera angles, do jump cuts and repetitions, etc. There should be no black-outs between scenes.

DESDEMONA was written as a tribute (i.e., "rip-off") to the infamous play, SHAKESPEARE THE SADIST by Wolfgang Bauer.

DESDEMONA

a play about a handkerchief

PROLOGUE

A spotlight in the dark, pin-pointing a white handkerchief lying on the ground. A second spotlight comes up on Emilia, who sees the handkerchief. She pauses, and then cautiously looks about to see if she is observed. Then, quickly, Emilia goes to the handkerchief, picks it up, stuffs the linen in her ample bodice, and exits. Blackout.

Scene 1

A mean, sparsely furnished back room with rough, white-washed walls. Upstage left there is a small heavy wooden back entrance. Another door, stage right, leads to the main rooms of the palace. There are a few benches lining the walls, littered with tools, baskets, leather bits, dirty laundry, etc. The walls bear dark wooden racks which neatly display farm and work equipment made of rough woods, leathers and chain.

In the center of the room, there is a crude work table with short benches. As the play begins, Desdemona is scattering items and clothing in the air, barely controlling a mounting hysteria. Emilia, dark, plump and plain, with a thick Irish brogue, watches, amused and disgusted at the mess her lady is making.

5

DESDEMONA.   Are you sure you didn't see it? The last time I remember holding it in my hand was last week in the arbor — you're sure you didn't see it?

EMILIA.   Aye —

DESDEMONA.   It looks like —

EMILIA.   — Like any body's handkerchief, savin' it has those dainty little strawberries on it. I never could be after embroiderin' a piece of linen with fancy work to wipe up the nose —

DESDEMONA.   — It's got to be here somewhere —

EMILIA.   — After you blow your nose in it, an' it's all heavy and wet, who's going to open the damn thing and look at the pretty stitches?

DESDEMONA.   Emilia — are you sure it didn't get "mixed up" somehow with your ... your things?

EMILIA.   And why should I be needin' your handkerchief when I'm wearing a plain, soft shift which works just as well? And failing that, the good Lord gave me sleeves....

DESDEMONA.   It's got to be here! *(Desdemona returns to her rampage of the room.)* Oh — skunk water! *(A man's undergarment is tossed into the air behind Desdemona's shoulder.)* Dog piddle!!

EMILIA.   I'm after telling you m'lady —

DESDEMONA.   Nonsense! It's got to be here! *(There is a crash of overturned chain. Desdemona's shifts are thrown into the air.)* God damn horse urine!!!

EMILIA.   It was dear, once upon the time, when m'lady was toddling about the palace, and all of us servants would be follerin' after, stooping to pick up all the pretty toys you'd be scatterin' —

DESDEMONA.   Emilia, please — I can not bear a sermon.

EMILIA.   There was the day the Senator your father gave you your first strand of pearls from the Indies — you were all of five — and your hand just plucked it from your neck — how you laughed to see us, Teresa, Maria and me, scrabbling on all fours like dogs after truffles, scooping up the rollin' pearls — *(There is a ripping noise.)*

DESDEMONA.   Oh, shit. *(Two halves of a sheet are pitched into the air.)*

EMILIA. But you're a married lady now; and when m'lord Othello gives you a thing, and tells you to be mindin' it, it's no longer dear to drop it willy nilly and expect me to be findin' it —

DESDEMONA.   Oh, piss and vinegar!! Where is the crappy little snot rag! *(Desdemona turns and sees Emilia sitting.)* You're not even helping! You're not looking!!

EMILIA.   Madam can be sure I've overturned the whole lot, two or three times.... It's a sight easier hunting for it when the place is tidy; when all is topsy-turvy, you can't tell a mouse dropping from a cow pie — *(Desdemona returns to the hunt: Emilia picks up the torn sheet.)* — Now see, this sheet here was washed this morning. Your husband, as you know, is fussy about his sheets; and while it was no problem to have them fresh each night in Venice — I could open the window and dunk them in the canal — here on Cyprus it takes two drooling orderlies to march six times down to the cistern and back again. *(Emilia regards the sheet carefully.)* It's beyond repair. And now that your husband commands fresh sheets, my Iago has got it in his head to be the lord as well; he's got to have fresh sheets each night for his unwashed feet.

DESDEMONA.   Emilia, please — I may puke. *(Desdemona, in frustration, stamps on the clothes she's strewn from the basket.)* It's got to be here, it's got to be here, it's got to be here — Emilia — Help me find it!

EMILIA.   You're wasting your time, m'lady. I know it's not here.

DESDEMONA.   *(Straightening herself.)* Right. And you knew this morning that my husband wasn't mad at me. Just a passing whim, you said.

EMILIA.   Ah, Miss Desdemona ... not even a midwife can foretell the perfidiosity of men.

DESDEMONA.   Give me strength. Perfidy.

EMILIA.   That, too.

DESDEMONA.   It can't have walked off on two feet!

EMILIA.   Mayhap m'lady dropped it.

DESDEMONA.   Oh, you're hopeless. No help at all. I'll find

it by myself. Go back to your washing and put your hands to use.
EMILIA.   Yes, m'lady.

Scene 2

Emilia and Desdemona. Emilia scrubs sheets.

DESDEMONA.   Will it come out?
EMILIA.   I've scrubbed many a sheet, but this is the worst in my career.... It's all that Bianca's fault. I paid her well for the blood, too. "And be sure," I says, "it's an old hen — one on its last gasp — young chick blood's no good for bridal sheets, it's the devil to come out. Madam's sheets," I says, "are the finest to be had in Venice, and we don't want them ruined and rotted from the stain." And Bianca swore, "I've an old hen on crutches that will wash out clear as a maidenhead or a baby's dropping." Ah, but that chick wasn't a week old. And what with it bakin' in the sun for a month now — but if anyone can, Mealy will scrub it virgin white again.
DESDEMONA.   Oh, hush about it. I can't stand to think on it ... barbaric custom. And my best sheets. Nobody displays bridal sheets on Cyprus.
EMILIA.   There aren't any virgins to be had on Cyprus.
DESDEMONA.   Half the garrison came to see those sheets flapping in the breeze.
EMILIA.   Why did the other half come?
DESDEMONA.   To pay their last respects to the chicken!
(*They laugh.*)

Scene 3

We hear Emilia, in a good humor, humming a tune suci as "When Irish Eyes Are Smiling."* Another clatter of heavy metal things being tossed onto the floor.

DESDEMONA.   JESUS! WHAT IS THIS?!
EMILIA.   *(In disbelief.)* You didn't find it! *(Desdemona crosses to Emilia, holding a long, crooked bit of iron with a wicked point.)*
DESDEMONA.   No — this!!
EMILIA.   'Tis a hoof-pick.
DESDEMONA.   A hoof-pick? What is it used for?
EMILIA.   After all your years of trotting m'lady's bum over field and farrow, and you've never laid your eyes on the like? When your mount picks up a stone in its foot, and it's deep, you take the pick and hold on tight to the hoof — and then you dig it in and down to the quick and pry it out —
DESDEMONA.   You dig *this* is? Good lord —
EMILIA.   Aye, takes a goodly amount of sweat and grease — it's work for a proper man, it is. *(Desdemona, absorbed in fondling the hoof-pick, stretches out on the table.)*
DESDEMONA.   Oh me, oh my — if I could find a man with just such a hoof-pick — he could pluck out my stone — eh, Emilia? *(They laugh.)* Emilia — does your husband Iago have a hoof-pick to match? *(Emilia turns and looks, then snorts.)*
EMILIA.   What, Iago? *(Desdemona puts her hand on the base and covers it.)*
DESDEMONA.   Well, then — this much?
EMILIA.   Please, mum! It's a matter o' faith between man and wife t —
DESDEMONA.   — Ahh — not that much, eh? *(Desdemona covers more of the pick.)* Like this?
EMILIA.   Miss Desdemona!
DESDEMONA.   Come now, Emilia — it's just us —

---

* See Special Note on copyright page.

EMILIA.   Some things are private!!

DESDEMONA.   It's only fair — I'm sure you know every detail about my lord —

EMILIA.   *(Shrugging.)* When the Master Piddles, a Servant holds the Pot —

DESDEMONA.   *(Persisting.)* This much 'hoof?'

EMILIA.   Not near as much as that!

DESDEMONA.   This much? *(Pause.)*

EMILIA.   *(Sour.)* Nay.

DESDEMONA.   Good God, Emilia, I'm running out of —

EMILIA.   — The wee-est pup of th' litter comes a'bornin' in the world with as much — *(Desdemona laughs.)* There. Is m'lady satisfied?

DESDEMONA.   Your secret's safe with me.

Scene 4

Emilia, scrubbing. Desdemona lies on her back on the table, feet propped up, absent-mindedly fondling the pick, and staring into space.

Scene 5

We hear the sound of Emilia, puffing and blowing. Lights up on Desdemona getting a pedicure.

DESDEMONA.   Where is she? It's getting late. He'll be back soon, and clamoring for me. He's been in a rotten mood lately.... Headaches, handkerchiefs, accusations — and of all people to accuse — Michael Cassio!

EMILIA.   The only one you haven't had —

DESDEMONA.   — And I don't want him, either. A prissy Florentine, that one is. Leave it to a cuckold to be jealous of a eunuch —

EMILIA. *(Crowing.)* — Bianca would die!
DESDEMONA.   Then we won't tell her what I said, will we?
(Emilia becomes quiet.) What Bianca does in her spare time is
her business. *(Emilia's face clearly indicates that what Bianca does
in her spare time is Emilia's business, too. Desdemona watches Emilia
closely.)* You don't much like Bianca, do you, Mealy? *(No response. Emilia blows on Desdemona's toes.)* Come on, now, tell me
frankly — why don't you like her?
EMILIA.   It's not for me to say ...
DESDEMONA.   Emilia!
EMILIA.   It's just that — no disrespect intented, m'lady, but
you shouldn't go a'rubbin' elbows with one o' her class.... Lie
down with hussies, get up with crabs ...
DESDEMONA.   Her sheets are clean. (P*ause.)* You've been
simmering over Bianca for some time, Mealy, haven't you?
EMILIA.   *(Rancorously.)* I don't much like to see m'lady, in
whose em-ploy I am, traipsing about in flopdens, doin' favors
for common sloppots — Bianca! Ha! She's so loose, so low,
that she's got to ad-ver-tise Wednesday Night Specials, half-
price for anything in uniform!
DESDEMONA.   Well, purge it out of your blood; Bianca will
soon be here —
EMILIA.   — Here! Why here? What if someone sees her
sneaking up to the back door? What will the women in town
say? A tart on a house call! How can I keep my head up
hanging out the wash and feedin' the pigs when her sort
comes sniffin' around —
DESDEMONA.   — She's coming to pay me for last
Tuesday's customers who paid on credit. And to arrange for
next Tuesday —
EMILIA.   *(Horrified.)* Not again! Once was enough — you're
not going there again! I thought to myself, she's a young un-
bridled colt, is Miss Desdemona — let her cool down her
blood — but to make it a custom! — I couldn't let you go
back again — risking disease and putting us all in danger —
DESDEMONA.   — Oh, tush, Mealy —
EMILIA.   — You listen to me, Miss Desdemona: Othello
will sooner or later find out that you're laying for Bianca, and

11

his black skin is goin' to blister off with rage!! Holy Jesus
Lord, why tempt a Venetian male by waving red capes? My
Iago would beat me for lookin' at the wrong end of an ass!
(Very worked up.) Your husband will find out and when he
does! When he does!! *(Emilia makes the noise and gesture of
throat cutting.)* And then! And then!! AIAIaiaiaiahhh!! My lady!!
What's to become of me! Your fateful hand-maid! Where will
I find another position in this pisshole harbour!
DESDEMONA.   Stop it, Mealy! Don't be ... silly, nothing will
happen to me. I'm the sort that will die in bed.
EMILIA.   *(Beseechingly.)* You won't leave your poor Mealy
stranded?
DESDEMONA.   You'll always have a position in this household.... Of some sort. *(Mealy's face turns to stone.)* Oh, come
now, Mealy, haven't I just promoted you?
EMILIA.   Oh, m'lady, I haven't forgot; not only your scullery
maid, but now your laundress as well! I am quite sensible of
the honor and the increase in pay — of two pence a week ...
(Emilia suddenly turns bright and cheery.) — and whiles we are
on the subject —
DESDEMONA.   — Oh, Christ, here it comes.
EMILIA.   But m'lady, last time an opening came up, you
promised to speak to your husband about it in Venice; I sup-
pose poor old Iago just slipped your mind —
DESDEMONA.   — Look, I did forget. Anyway, I recom-
mended Cassio for my husband's lieutenant. An unfortunate
choice. But that subject is closed.
EMILIA.   Yes, mum. *(Emilia starts to return to her laundry. There
is a knock at the door, and Desdemona brightens.)*
DESDEMONA.   There she is! Emilia, let Bianca in — No, no
wait — *(To Mealy's annoyance, Desdemona arranges herself in a
casual tableau. The knock repeats. Desdemona signals Emilia to go
answer the door. Emilia exits through the door to the palace, and
then quickly returns.)*
EMILIA.   M'lady, it's your husband. He's waiting for you
outside.
DESDEMONA.   *(Frightened.)* Husband?... Shhhittt ...
(Desdemona pauses, arranges her face into an insipid, fluttering in-

nocence, then girlishly runs to the door. She flings it open, and disappears through the door. We hear a breathless Desdemona, off.) Otello! *(And then, we hear the distinct sound of a very loud slap. A pause, and Desdemona returns, closes the door behind her, holding her cheek. She is on the brink of tears. She and Emilia look at each other, and then Emilia looks away.)*

Scene 6

Desdemona and Emilia. Desdemona frantically searches.

DESDEMONA.   It's got to be somewhere!! — Are yóu quite sure —
EMILIA.   — Madam can be sure I overlooked the whole lot several times.
DESDEMONA.   Um, Emilia — should, should you have "accidentally" taken it — not that I'm suggesting theft in the slightest — but should it have by mistake slipped in with some of your things — your return of it will merit a reward, and all of my gratitude. *(Desdemona tries to appear casual.)* Not that the thing itself is worth anything — it's a pittance of musty linen — but still ...
EMILIA.   *(With dignity.)* I've never taken a thing, acc-idently or not. I don't make no "acc-idents." Mum, I've looked everywhere. Everywhere. *(Quietly.)* Is m'lord clamoring about it much? *(They eye each other. Pause.)*
DESDEMONA.   Which position, Mealy?
EMILIA.   *(Puzzled.)* Which position?
DESDEMONA.   For your husband.
EMILIA.   Oh, Miss Desdemona! I won't forget all your —
DESDEMONA.   — Yes, yes, I'm sure. What opening?
EMILIA.   It's ever so small a promotion, and so quite equal to his merits. He's ensign third-class, but the budget's ensign second-class.
DESDEMONA.   Very well, the budget office. Can he write

13

and account and do — whatever it is that they do with the budget?

EMILIA.   Oh, yes — he's clever enough at that.

DESDEMONA.   I really don't understand your mentality. Emilia. You're forever harping on how much you detest the man. Why do you beg for scraps of promotion for him? Don't you hate him?

EMILIA.   I — I — *(With relish.)* I *despise* him.

DESDEMONA.   Then?

EMILIA.   You see, miss, for us in the bottom ranks, when man and wife hate each other, what is left in a lifetime of marriage but to save and scrimp, plot and plan? The more I'd like to put some nasty rat-ridder in his stew, the more I think of money — and he thinks the same. One of us will drop first, and then, what's left, saved and earned, under the mattress for th' other one? I'd like to rise a bit in the world, and women can only do that through their mates — no matter what class buggers they all are. I says to him each night — I long for the day you make me a lieutenant's widow!

Scene 7

Emilia and Desdemona. We hear the sounds of scrubbing between the scenes.

DESDEMONA.   Please, my dear Emilia — I can count on you, can't I? As one closest to my confidence?

EMILIA.   Oh, m'lady — I ask no greater joy than to be close to your ladyship —

DESDEMONA.   Then tell me — have you heard anything about me? Why does Othello suspect Cassio?

EMILIA.   Oh, no, m'lady, he surely no longer suspects Cassio; I instructed Iago to talk him out of that bit of fancy, which he did, risking my lord's anger at no little cost to his own career; but all for you, you know!

DESDEMONA.   You haven't heard of anything else?

EMILIA.   No Ma'am. *(But as Desdemona is to Emilia's back, Emilia drops a secret smile into the wash bucket. Emilia raises her head again, though, with a sincere, servile face, and turns to Desdemona.)* But if I did know anything, you can be sure that you're the first to see the parting of my lips about it —

DESDEMONA.   Yes, I know. You've been an extremely faithful, hard-working servant to me, Emilia, if not a confidante. I've noticed your merits, and when we return to Venice — well — you may live to be my *fille de chambre* yet.

EMILIA.   *(Not quite sure what a* fille de chambre *is.)* I'm very grateful, I'm sure.

DESDEMONA.   Yes — you deserve a little reward, I think — *(Emilia's face brightens in expectancy.)* — I'll see if I can wheedle another tuppence out of my husband each week ... *(Emilia droops.)*

EMILIA.   *(Listlessly.)* Every little tiny bit under the mattress helps, I always says to myself. *(A pause. Desdemona paces, comes to a decision.)*

DESDEMONA.   Mealy — do you like the dressing gown you've been mending?

EMILIA.   It's a lovely piece of work, that is, Miss. I've always admired your dresses ...

DESDEMONA.   Yesss ... yes, but isn't it getting a bit dingy? Tattered around the hem?

EMILIA.   Not that anyone would notice; it's a beautiful gown, m'lady ...

DESDEMONA.   Yes, you're right. I was going to give it to you, but maybe I'll hang on to it a bit longer ... *(Emilia, realizing her stupidity, casts an avaricious, yet mournful look at the gown that was almost hers.)*

EMILIA.   Oh, m'lady.... It's — it's certainly a lovely cloth, and there's a cut to it that would make one of them boy actors shapely ...

DESDEMONA.   *(Peeved at the analogy.)* Hmmmm — tho', come to think of it, it would fit Bianca much neater, I think ...

EMILIA.   Bianca! Bianca! She's got the thighs of a milch cow, m'lady!

DESDEMONA.   *(Amused.)* I've never noticed. *(Emilia, sulking again, vigorously scrubs. In conciliation.)* No, come to think of it, I believe you are right — it's not really Bianca's fashion. It's all yours. After tonight.

EMILIA.   Oh, Miss Desdemona!!

Scene 8

The same. In the darkness we hear Emilia singing a hymn: "la la la la — Jesus; la-la-la-la — sword; la-la-la-la — crucifix; la-la-la-la — word." Lights come up on Desdemona lying stretched out on the table, her throat and head arched over its edge, upside down. A pause.

DESDEMONA.   You really think his temper today was only some peeve?

EMILIA.   I'm sure of it; men get itchy heat rash in th' crotch, now and then; they get all snappish, but once they beat us, it's all kisses and presents the next morning — well, for the first year or so.

DESDEMONA.   My dear mate is much too miserly to give me anything but his manhood. The only gift he's given me was a meager handkerchief with piddling strawberries stitched on it, and look how he's carrying on because I've lost it! He guards his purse strings much dearer than his wife.

EMILIA.   I'm sure my Lord will be waitin' up for you to come to bed. Full o' passion, and embracin' and makin' a fool o' himself — You just see if your Mealy isn't right.

DESDEMONA.   Yes, of course you're right. Good old Mealy, I don't know what I'd do without your good common sense. Oh, it's the curse of aristocratic blood — I feel full of whims and premonitions —

EMILIA.   Perhaps it was something m'lady et?

DESDEMONA.   *(First she smiles — then she laughs.)* Yes — that must be it! *(Desdemona laughs again. Mealy can't understand what is so funny.)*

16

Scene 9

Emilia and Desdemona.

EMILIA.   Ambassador Ludovico gave me a message and is wantin' a response.

DESDEMONA.   What does my cousin want? *(Emilia digs into her bodice.)*

EMILIA.   It's somewhere in here ... wait — *(Emilia searches.)*

DESDEMONA.   Oh, good Lord, Mealy, you could lose it in there! *(Desdemona runs to Emilia, peers in her bosom, and starts to tickle her.)*

EMILIA.   Miss Desde — ! Wait, now — no, STOP!! Here it is now — *(Emilia finds a folded paper. She hands it to Desdemona, and then peers over Desdemona's shoulder.)*

DESDEMONA.   *(Sighing.)* Oh, Ludovico, Ludovico. "Deeply desiring the favor, etceteras." "... Impatient until I can at last see you in private, throwing off the Robes of State to appear as your humble friend." He's just too tiresome.

EMILIA.   What response are you wanting me to give?

DESDEMONA.   Oh, I don't know. Let the old lecher wait. I told him it was entirely past between us, and then he bribes his way into being appointed Ambassador! *(Desdemona in a loquacious mood. Emilia gives her a rub-down.)* Ah, Emilia, I should have married Ludovico after all. There's a man who's always known the worth of ladies of good blood! A pearl for a pinch, a broach for a breast, and for a maiden-head ... *(Desdemona breaks into laughter.)* Ah, that was a lover!

EMILIA.   I don't know how those sainted sisters could let such is-sagnations go on in their convent —

DESDEMONA.   — assignations. Really, Emilia, you're quite hopeless. However can I, the daughter of a senator, live with a washerwoman as *fille de chambre*? All fashionable Venice will howl. You must shrink your vowels and enlarge your vocabulary.

EMILIA.   Yes, mum. As-signations, as it were. *(Muttering.)* If it were one o' my class, I could call it by some names I could pronounce. I've put many a copper in their poor box, in times past, thinkin' them sisters of charity in a godly house. Not no more. They won't get the parings of my potatoes from me, runnin' a society house of ass-ignations!

DESDEMONA.   Oh, those poor, dear sisters. I really don't think they knew anything about the informal education their convent girls receive; for one thing, I believe myopia is a prerequisite for Holy Orders. Have you ever noticed how nuns squint? *(Beat.)* Each Sunday in convent we were allowed to take visitors to chapel; under their pious gaze Ludovico and I would kneel — and there I could devote myself to doing him *à la main* — *(Desdemona gestures.)* — right in the pew! They never noticed! Sister Theresa did once remark that he was a man excessively fond of prayer.

Scene 10

Emilia's credo.

EMILIA.   It's not right of you, Miss Desdemona, to be forever cutting up on the matter of my beliefs. I believe in the Blessed Virgin, I do, and the Holy Fathers and the Sacraments of the Church, and I'm not one to be ashamed of admittin' it. It goes against my marrow, it does, to hear of you, a comely lass from a decent home, giving hand jobs in the pew; but I says to myself, Emilia, I says, you just pay it no mind, and I go about my business. And if I take a break on the Sabbath each week, to light a candle and say a bead or two for my em-ployers, who have given me and my husband so much, and who need the Virgin's love and protection, then where's the harm, say I? *(Breath. Emilia gets carried away.)* Our Lady has seen me through four and ten years of matreemony, with my bugger o' a mate, and that's no mean feat. Four and ten years, she's heard poor Mealy's cries, and stopped me from rising from my bed with my pillow in my hand to end his ugly snores 'til Gabriel — *(Emilia stops and composes herself.)* — Ah, Miss Desdemona, if you only knew the peace and love

18

Our Lady brings! She'd help you, mum, if you only kneeled real nice and said to her — and said — *(Emilia can't find the words that such a sinner as Desdemona should say as polite salutation to Our Lady. Desdemona, erupts into laughter.)*

Scene 11

Emilia eats her lunch. Desdemona plays in a desultory fashion with a toy. Then, frightened.

DESDEMONA.   Emilia — have you ever deceived your husband Iago?
EMILIA.   *(With a derisive snort.)* That's a good one. Of course not, miss — I'm an honest woman.
DESDEMONA.   What does honesty have to do with adultery? Every honest man I know is an adulterer ... *(Pause.)* Have you ever thought about it?
EMILIA.   What is there to be thinkin' about? It's enough trouble once each Saturday night, than to be lookin' for it. I'd never cheat, never, not for all the world I wouldn't.
DESDEMONA.   The world's a huge thing for so small a vice.
EMILIA.   Not my world, thank you — mine's tidy and neat and I aim to keep it that way.
DESDEMONA.   Oh, the world! Our world's narrow and small, I'll grant you — but there are other worlds — worlds that we married women never get to see.
EMILIA.   Amen — and don't need to see, I should add.
DESDEMONA.   If you've never seen the world, how would you know? Women are clad in purdah, we decent, respectable matrons, from the cradle to the altar to the shroud ... bridled with linen, blinded with lace.... These very walls are purdah.
EMILIA.   I don't know what this thing called "purr-dah" means, but if it stands for dressing up nice, I'm all for it ...
DESDEMONA.   I remember the first time I saw my husband and I caught a glimpse of his skin, and oh, how I thrilled. I thought — aha — a man of a different color. From another

19

world and planet. I thought — if I marry this strange dark man, I can leave this narrow little Venice with its whispering piazzas behind — I can escape and see other worlds. (*Pause.*) But under that exotic facade was a porcelain white Venetian.

EMILIA.   There's nothing wrong with Venice; I don't understand why Madam's all fired up to catch Cyprus Syph and exotic claps.

DESDEMONA.   Of course you don't understand. But I think Bianca does. She's a free woman — a new woman, who can make her own living in the world — who scorns marriage for the lie that it is.

EMILIA.   I don't know where Madam's getting this new woman hog-wash, but no matter how you dress up a cow, she's still got udders. Bianca's the eldest one of six girls, with teeth so horsy she could clean 'em with a hoof pick, and so simple she has to ply the trade she does! That's what your Miss Bianca is!

DESDEMONA.   Bianca is nothing of the sort. She and I share something common in our blood — that desire to know the world. I lie in the blackness of the room at her establishment ... on sheets that are stained and torn by countless nights. And the men come into that pitch-black room — men of different sizes and smells and shapes, with smooth skin — with rough skin, with scarred skin. And they spill their seed into me, Emilia — seed from a thousand lands, passed down through generations of ancestors, with genealogies that cover the surface of the globe. And I simply lie still there in the darkness, taking them all into me; I close my eyes and in the dark of my mind — oh, how I travel!

Scene 12

Emilia and Desdemona. Desdemona is recklessly excited.

EMILIA.   You're leaving?!! Your husband?!!

DESDEMONA.   It's a possibility!

EMILIA.   Miss Desdemona, you've been taking terrible chances before but now — if my Lord catches you giving him th' back wind, he'll be after murdering both of us for sure —

DESDEMONA.   Where's my cousin Ludovico? Is he in his room?

EMILIA.   He said he was turnin' in early to get some rest before th' morning —

DESDEMONA.   Yes — he'll catch the first tide back. Well, there's no harm in trying.

EMILIA.   Trying what!

DESDEMONA.   Trying on the robes of the penitent daughter. Ludovico can surely see how detestable this island, this marriage, this life is for me. *(Desdemona has worked herself to the point of tears. Then she smiles.)* Perhaps a few tears would move him to intercede with my father on my behalf. If the disgrace of eloping with a Moor is too great for Venetian society, a small annual allowance from Papa and I promise never to show my face in town; and then ... who knows.... Paris! Yes, I'll go write Ludovico a note right away, asking to see him tonight. — Mealy — just in case — could you pack a few things for me?

EMILIA.   And what if your husband discovers —

DESDEMONA.   I'll leave first thing in the morning.

EMILIA.   If I may make so bold to suggest —

DESDEMONA.   What, what —

EMILIA.   That you by all means sleep with your husband tonight. So's he won't suspect anything. While you and he lie together, and if your cousin agrees, Mealy could pack up your things quiet-like in your chamber.

DESDEMONA.   Yes, that's good. My life rests on your absolute discretion, Emilia.

21

EMILIA.   No one will hear a peep out o' me. But my lady —
DESDEMONA.   Now what is it?
EMILIA.   What becomes of me?
DESDEMONA.   Oh, good heavens, Mealy — I can't think of trivia at a time like this. *(Smoothly.)* I tell you what. Be a good girl, pack my things — and of course, should I leave tomorrow, I can't very well smuggle you on board, too — but I will send for you within the week. And your services will be remembered in Venice; with freer purse strings — who knows? Eh, my *fille de chambre?* *(At this sop to her feelings, Emilia becomes fierce.)*
EMILIA.   That won't do, m'lady. If you leave me behind, I'll not see you again, as your laundress, much less as your "fee der schomer" — *(Desdemona, realizing the power that Emilia now has, kneels beside Emilia.)*
DESDEMONA.   All right. I'll intercede with my cousin on your behalf. I'll plead with him to take you, too. But I can't promise anything. Are you sure it's what you want? *(Emilia nods.)* You'd leave your husband behind? *(Emilia nods vigorously.)* Then — not a word. *(Desdemona rises, and in turning to go.)* Oh, Emilia — since you're just dawdling over that laundry — why not stop and peel some potatoes for Cook. When my husband comes in, he'll want his usual snack of chips before he turns in — just the way he likes them — *(Desdemona shudders.)* — greasy.
EMILIA.   But Miss, it's not my place no more to peel potatoes! I'm promoted now! I'm no mere *(With disgust.)* — SCULLERY MAID.
DESDEMONA.   Now, Mealy, just this once —
EMILIA.   — You said I wouldn't have to do potatoes anymore!
DESDEMONA.   *(Harshly.)* — I can leave you rotting on Cyprus all together, you know. Do as you're told. Peel the potatoes, and then look sharp and have that wash on the line by the time I return. Do I make myself clear?
EMILIA.   Yes, m'lady.
DESDEMONA.   *(Sweetly.)* And Emilia, dear — if Bianca comes when I'm gone, let me know immediately — I'll be in

my chamber.

EMILIA. Very good, Miss Desdemona. *(Desdemona exits. Emilia grudgingly gets up, and finds the barrel of potatoes. On the bench there is a paring knife. Emilia brings everything back to the table, sits, and begins paring potatoes — venting her resentment on gouging out eyes, and stripping the skin from a potato as if flaying a certain mistress alive. Then, she snorts out in contempt.)* Fee der shomber! *(Then Emilia pauses and wonders if Desdemona might not be for real in her offer — and questions the empty room with.)* Feeyah der schomber? *(Before Emilia's eyes, she visualizes splendid dresses, the command of a household of subservient maids, a husbandless existence — all the trappings that go with the title. Emilia begins energetically, resolutely and obediently to slice the potatoes.)*

Scene 13

Emilia is hanging up the wash. Bianca knocks several times. Then enters.

BIANCA. Gaw Blimey!

EMILIA. And where is' you've lost your manners? Lettin' the door ajar and leavin' in drafts and the pigs —

BIANCA. Aw'm sorry, Aw'm sure ... *(Bianca closes the door. Hesitates, and then with friendly strides, goes towards the clothesline.)* 'Ow do, Emilia!

EMILIA. I'd be doin' a lot better if ye'd stop your gaddin' and lend a hand with these things.

BIANCA. Oh. Right you are, then. *(Bianca goes briskly to the clothesline, and works. Silence as the women empty the basket. Emilia leaves Bianca to finish and starts in on her sewing. Pause.)* Well, it's — it ain't 'arf swank 'ere, eh? *(Bianca indicates the room.)*

EMILIA. *(Snorts.)* Swank? What, this? This is only the *back* room. The palace is through those doors —

BIANCA. Oh. Well, it's swank for a back room wotever it 'tis. Aw niver got to see it much; the Guv'nor in the owld days didn't let me near, said Aw made the men tomdoodle on their shifts; like as they'd be dis-tracted by me atomy. Aw think it's sweet o' him to gi' me such credit; me atomy ain't that bleedin' jammy — but then, the owld Guv was the first to gi' me the sheeps' eye 'imself — very sweet on me, 'e was. So you see, Aw'd niver got close to the place before. Aw fink it's swank!

EMILIA.   *(Icily.)* I'm sure you do.

BIANCA.   Yes, it's quite — wot do ye call it — lux-i-o-rious.

EMILIA.   Lux-i-o-ri-us!! If I was you, I'd large my voc-abulary, an' shrink me vowels.

BIANCA.   *(Offended.)* 'Ere now! Wot bus'ness is me vowels to you?! Leave me vowels alone —

EMILIA.   — I'm after talking about your voc-abulary — your patter — not your reg-ularity.

BIANCA.   Oh. *(Keeping up a friendly front with difficulty.)* Right. Well, then, is Desdemona 'ere?

EMILIA.   *(Sharply.)* Who?

BIANCA.   Uh — Des-de-mona ...

EMILIA.   Is it m'lady you're referrin' to as if she were your mess mate?

BIANCA.   Look 'ere — Aw'm only doin' as Aw was towld. She tells me to call her Desdemona, and she says Aw was to call and settle up accounts for last Tuesday night for those johns who paid on tick — oh, you know, who paid on credit, as yew la-de-da Venetians would say.

EMILIA.   *(Softly hissed.)* You listen to me, lassie: you're riding for a fall the likes of which you never got paid for by your fancy men. The mistress of this house is not at home, nor will be to the likes of you. What m'lady does in the gutter is her own business, same as yours, but what happens here is the common buzz of all.

BIANCA.   *(Stunned.)* Wot! Miss Desdemona herself is callin' us mates; Aw niver —

EMILIA.   — then she's gullin' you, as sure as 'tis she's gullin' that ass of a husband who's so taken with her; but let me tell you, you'll go the way like all the other fancies she's had in Venice.... *I* should know. We all of us servants in her father's house talked on end about Miss Desdemona. — For a time, she wanted to be a saint, yes! A nun with the sisters of mercy. At age 12 she was washin' the courtyard stones for penance, with us wiping up behind her. Then she was taken with horses, thank Jesus, and left sainthood behind — and then in turn again, she thought she was dyin' — stopped eating, and moped, and talked all dreamy and a little balmy-like — until her father finally saw sense and sent her to the convent to be bred out of her boredom. You're nothin' but the latest whim, a small town floozy with small town slang, and if she's lucky, she'll tire of you before the master finds out. *(Significantly.)* *If* she's lucky.

BIANCA.	*(Somewhat subdued.)* So wot am Aw t'do, Emilia? Aw arsks you —

EMILIA.	— Then ask me by "Miss Emilia" to you — *(With great dignity.)* I'll have you know, I've hereby been promoted to "fee der shimber" and if I was you, I'd keep on my right side.

BIANCA.	*(Impressed, scared.)* Oh — "fee dar shimber" — Aw niver met one o' those before — Aw arsks yer pardon, Miss Emilia, Aw'm sure.

EMILIA.	That's a bit of all right. You just listen to me: I know what side of me bread is buttered; behind this whimsycal missus is a power of a master — so you mind yourself; the smell of your sin's goin' to catch m'lord's whiffin' about, and he's as jealous as he's black. If m'lord Othello had a mind to it, he could have that little lollin' tongue of yours cut clean out of your head, with none of the citizens of Cyprus to say him nay. And then what would you do for your customers! If he catched you degineratin' his wife —

BIANCA.	*(Starting to cry with fear.)* Aw swear, Miss Emilia, Aw'm not degineratin' m'lady; we was just mates, that's wot; if Missus Desdemona wants to lark and gull her smug of a husband, that's her business, then, ain't it? Aw done as she towld me, an' that's all — she's a good lady, an' all, and Aw've just been friendly-like to her —

EMILIA.	— Don't be a little fool hussy. There's no such creature, two, three, or four-legged, as "friend" betwixt ladies

of leisure and ladies of the night. And as long as there be
men with one member but two minds, there's no such thing
as friendship between women. An' that's that. So turn yourself
around, go out and close the door behind you, and take all
traces of the flophouse with you — includin' your tall tales
about your "friendships" with ladies —
BIANCA.   *(Anger finally conquering fear.)* You can call me wot
you like, but Aw'm no liar! Aw'm as 'onest a woman as
yerself! And wot's more, mebbe you can wipe yer trotters on
women who have to crack their crusts by rolling blokes in
Venice, but 'ere it's differnt. — Aw have a place 'ere and
Aw'm not ashamed t'own it — Aw'm nice to the wives in
town, and the wives in town are rather nice to me. Aw'm
doin' them favors by puttin' up wif their screwy owld men,
and Aw like me job! The only ponk Aw has to clean up is me
own. *(Starts to leave but.)* — And wot's more, Aw likes yer lady,
whefer you think so or not. She can see me as Aw am, and
not arsk for bowin' and scrapin' — she don't have to be
nobby, 'cause she's got breedin', and she don't mind liking
me for me own self — wifout th' nobby airs of yer Venetian
washerwomen! Aw'm at home 'ere in my place — you, you
Venetian washerdonna — you're the one out o' yer element!
*(Bianca stalks to the door, but before she can reach it, Desdemona
enters.)*
DESDEMONA.   Emilia.

Scene 14

The same. Desdemona, Emilia and Bianca.

DESDEMONA.   Emilia. I thought I told you to tell me the
instant Miss Bianca arrived. Well?
EMILIA.   I didn't want to be botherin' m'lady with the ambassador —
DESDEMONA.   — I want none of your excuses for your
rudeness to our guest. My dear Bianca! I've been waiting im-

patiently — I could have just died of boredom. *(Desdemona bestows a warm hug on Bianca.)* — May I kiss you? *(Desdemona "kisses" Bianca by pressing both sides of their cheeks together.)*

BIANCA. *(Stammering.)* Aw'm not worthy of it, m'lady —

DESDEMONA. Oh, Bianca, so stiff and formal! — What have I done that you should be so angry with me?

BIANCA. *(Quickly.)* Nofing! Your lady's been all kindness to me ... but mayhap ... Aw'm not the sort o' mate for one o' your company!

DESDEMONA. Nonsense! I'll decide my own friendships ... *(Desdemona looks meaningfully at Emilia. To Bianca.)* You must excuse my entertaining you in such a crude barn of a room; my room's much cozier, but I don't know when my ... my ... "smug" — is that right? *(Bianca nods.)* — when he'll return. *(Desdemona laughs.)* Right now Othello's out in the night somewhere playing Roman Orator to his troops. *(Desdemona guides Bianca to the table: they sit side by side.)* Emilia.... Ask Miss Bianca if she'd like some wine. *(To Bianca.)* It's really quite good, my dear. *(Emilia glumly approaches Bianca.)*

EMILIA. Well, are you wantin' any?

DESDEMONA. Emilia! "Would you care for some wine, Miss Bianca?"

EMILIA. *(Deep breath, red.)* "Would you care for some wine, Miss Bianca?"

BIANCA. Why thank you — D-desdemona, Aw could do w' a sneaker —

DESDEMONA. *(Laughs.)* How I love the way you talk!... Emilia, fetch the wine and two goblets. That will be all.

EMILIA. Yes, mum. *(Emilia exits and Bianca relaxes.)*

DESDEMONA. My poor Bianca; has Emilia been berating you?

BIANCA. Well, Aw don't know about that, but she's been takin' me down a bit. Aw don't thinks she likes me very much.

DESDEMONA. Oh, what does that matter! Why should you want her friendship — you don't have to care what anyone thinks about you — you're a totally free woman, able to snap your fingers in any one's face!

BIANCA.   Yea, that's wot all right — but still, Aw likes people to like me.
DESDEMONA.   Oh, well, you mustn't mind Emilia. She's got a rotten temper because her husband — her "smug" — is such a rotter. Oh, Iago! *(Desdemona shudders.)* Do you know him?
BIANCA.   *(Smiling, looking away.)* Aw know 'im by sight —
DESDEMONA.   You know the one, then — the greasy little man. He's been spilling his vinegar into her for fourteen years of marriage, until he's corroded her womb from the inside out — and every day she becomes more and more hallowed out, just — just a vessel of vinegar herself.
BIANCA.   *(Disturbed.)* Wot a funny way of lookin' at it —
(Bianca is bewildered.)

Scene 15

Bianca and Desdemona.

BIANCA.   So you don't fancy Iago, then, do you?
DESDEMONA.   Detest him. But of course, I don't have anything to do with him — I only need suffer his wife's company. Poor old Mealy —
BIANCA.   — "Mealy?" *(Bianca laughs, her fear of Emilia diminishing.)*
DESDEMONA.   Yes, I've nicknamed her that, because I suspect it annoys her. Still, it fits. *(Desdemona and Bianca giggle.)* Alas, when Othello and I eloped it was on such short notice and my husband's so stingy with salary that the only maid I could bring was my father's scullery maid.
BIANCA.   Yer scullery maid! Not — not yer — wot-de-ye-call it — "Fee dah — Feyah der — "
DESDEMONA.   *"Fille de Chambre!"* Heavens, no! I keep her in line with the prospect of eventual advancement, but she's much too unsuitable for that — why she doesn't speak a word of French, and she's crabby to boot. Still, she's devoted and

that makes up for all the rest.

BIANCA.   Wot makes you fink she's devoted?

DESDEMONA.   Ah, a good mistress knows the secret
thoughts of her maids. She's devoted.

BIANCA.   Well, it's a cooshy enough way to crack a crust ...

DESDEMONA.   Crack a crust?

BIANCA.   Oh — beg yer pardon; Aw mean t'earn a livin' —

DESDEMONA.   *(Enthralled.)* "Crack a crust!" How clever you
are, Bianca!

Scene 16

*Desdemona, Bianca and Emilia. Emilia stands before
Desdemona, bearing a pitcher and two mugs on a tray.*

EMILIA.   Wine, m'lady ...

DESDEMONA.   Ah, excellent. *(Emilia serves Desdemona first
with all the grace she can muster; then she negligently pushes the
wine in the direction of Bianca.)*

BIANCA.   Thank you, Mealy.

DESDEMONA.   *(Toasting Bianca.)* Now, then: to our friendship!

BIANCA.   T' yer 'ealth — *(Desdemona delicately sips her wine,
as Bianca belts it down so that the wine trickles from the corner of
her mouth. Emilia is aghast. As Bianca wipes her mouth with her
hand, she notices Emilia's shock and blurts.)* 'Scuse me guttlin' it
down me gob —

DESDEMONA.   Oh, tush, Bianca. Mealy, haven't you mending to carry on with? *(Emilia silently seats herself apart and picks
up the drawers.)* I tell you, Bianca, it's a disgrace. My husband
refuses to buy new linen for his drawers, so Emilia must constantly mend the old. *(Confidentially.)* He's constantly tearing
his crotch-hole somehow.

BIANCA.   *(Amused.)* And how does that happen?

DESDEMONA.   *(Demurely.)* I have no idea. — More wine,
dear?

Scene 17

The same. Bianca and Desdemona, drinking. Emilia sews.

DESDEMONA.   How about another ... round?
BIANCA.   All right, then. *(Desdemona pours generously.)* — But not so much! Aw could get lushy easy. *(Bianca sips her wine: Desdemona knocks it back, and wipes her mouth with her hand. They laugh.)*

Scene 18

Desdemona and Bianca, drinking. They are giggling help-lessly, spluttering. Emilia sews. Desdemona starts to choke on her wine from laughing.

Scene 19

The same. Desdemona and Bianca try to control themselves. Then Desdemona holds up the hoof pick, and Bianca and Desdemona explode in raucous laughter. Emilia is furious.

Scene 20

The same.

BIANCA.   Listen, luvs, where's yer five-minute lodging?
DESDEMONA.   My ... what?
BIANCA.   Yer Drury Lane? Yer — where's yer bleedin' crapper! Yew know — where do yew make water?
EMILIA.   M'lady makes her water in a hand-painted Limoge

pot, a holy sight with angels havin' a grand time — it's not for the like of you!

DESDEMONA.   There's an outhouse in the back by the shed ... careful of the muck and the pigs.

BIANCA.   'Ta. Be back in a few.... Aw've got t' go see a bloke about a horse. *(Bianca exits.)*

EMILIA.   And you're after havin' yourself a proper time.

DESDEMONA.   Oh; Mealy, I'm sorry — we were just having fun —

EMILIA.   At my husband's expense. You finagled that out o' me, and then you went and told it to My Lady of the Public Square ...

DESDEMONA.   It.... It just ... slipped out. *(Desdemona goes into another gale of laughter. Then.)* — Mealy — I'm going to ask her about Cassio!

EMILIA.   Why must you be knowin' every man's size?! *(Desdemona laughs again.)*

DESDEMONA.   — No, I mean I'm going to tell her that Othello suspects him.

EMILIA.   Are you daft from the wine?

DESDEMONA.   Why not? Maybe we can get to the bottom of this ...

EMILIA.   Why is it mattering? Tomorrow morning we're leaving with the ambassador —

DESDEMONA.   — Yes, yes, but I can find out why —

EMILIA.   — I don't understand why m'lady is in such a rush to havin' her throat slashed our last night on Cyprus —

DESDEMONA.   — Look, I'll just tell her that my husband is under some false impression, and ask her for —

EMILIA.   — And why should she be believin' you?

DESDEMONA.   She'll believe me! She'll believe me because ... I'll give her ... I'll give her ... my word of honor.

EMILIA.   And just how much goat cheese does that buy at market? — I know the world! I've seen flesh buckets fightin' for their fancy men in the streets in Venice, and a pretty sight it was!

DESDEMONA.   Oh, Mealy —

EMILIA.   — You'll be bleedin' on the wrong time of the

31

month! Those trullies, all of them, carry slashers down in their boots — *(Bianca throws open the door and sticks her head in; Emilia and Desdemona are startled.)*
BIANCA.   Did-jew miss me?

Scene 21

Bianca, Desdemona and Emilia.

BIANCA.   'Ere now — let me settle w' you fer Tuesday night — let's see ... *(Bianca rummages in a pocket of her dress.)* It were six pence a john, at ten johns makes fer ... five bob, an' tuppence fer tips. *(Emilia gasps.)*
DESDEMONA.   I can hear what you're thinking Mealy — Holy Mother, I made more in twenty minutes than you do in a week of washing!
EMILIA.   Five bob ...
DESDEMONA.   How large now the world for so small a vice, eh, Mealy?
EMILIA.   I'm — I'm not to be tempted, Miss Desdemona.
DESDEMONA.   Brave girl!
BIANCA.   'Ere's the brass ready. Tuppence for tips is bleedin'-well for a Tuesday.
DESDEMONA.   Really?
BIANCA.   It so be as how Wednesday is pay-day 'ere; Tuesday nights are the cooshiest layin', but the stingiest payin' —
EMILIA.   Aye, "Men earns their money like Horses and spends it like Asses" ...
DESDEMONA.   Never mind Mealy, Bianca; she's over there calculating what price fidelity. Now about next week —
EMILIA.   — You two can cackle with laughter at me if you like, but it's a duty for me to stop your ladyship from gettin' into danger —
BIANCA.   *(Offended.)* Danger! Wot danger! She helped me out on me Adam an' Eve Night — there's no danger; Aw gave her me lambs; the feisty, firkin' lads come on th' other

nights, not on Tuesday. It don't take no elbow grease; Tuesday's just lying back and Adam an' Evein' it —

EMILIA. I don't understand your "Adam and Eve" and I don't think I want to ...

DESDEMONA. Oh yes you do, Mealy; "Adam and Eve" is what you and Iago did on your wedding night ...

BIANCA. She just might fink it means fallin' asleep — *(Emilia vigorously stitches the linen.)*

DESDEMONA. She's right, tho', Bianca, she's only trying to protect me; how about if we leave next Tuesday night open. If I can sneak away into the darkness of your boudoir, then I'll send word by Emilia —

BIANCA. Right, then, but you understand me, Miss Desdemona, there'll be no firsky johns when you comes clandecently; just the meek ones who are low on pocket-brass, or the stingy-mingy-gits who don't want to pay for nothin' wild; an' there'll be a fresh bed, an' the room so dark that your own husband wouldn't know you —

DESDEMONA. — Oh, Bianca — what a thought — do you think he'd come? I'd die for sure — *(Desdemona laughs.)* — And wouldn't he be mad if he'd paid for what he got for free at home!!

BIANCA. Well, the room's bleedin' black — blacker than he is. *(Bianca and Emilia laugh together; Desdemona is affronted.)*

DESDEMONA. I beg your pardon?

BIANCA. No, no — all my Tuesday johns are reg'lars — Aw know 'em all. So if you want, let me know — it'll be treacle next to wot Aw had today —

DESDEMONA. — Do tell, Bianca —

EMILIA. — Hasn't m'lady had enough —

DESDEMONA. — Oh, hush, Mealy — just mend your crotches, and don't listen.

BIANCA. All right, then. Aw have this one john who comes once a week for an L & B —

DESDEMONA. "L & B?"

BIANCA. In th' Life, it's known as a lam an' brim — first they lam you, an' mayhap you lam them, then you brim 'em — *(Desdemona looks blank.)* You know — first they beat you, an' then you beat them, and then you give 'em wotever — an Adam an' Eve, or a Sunny-side Over —

DESDEMONA.   *(Dawning.)* You mean men actually pay to beat you? And to be beaten?

BIANCA.   Oh, well, it costs 'em a pretty penny, Aw can tell you; there's nothin' doin' for less than two bob.

DESDEMONA.   *(Eyes wide.)* My. Well, carry on.

BIANCA.   Well, there's this one john, an owld mate, who's been on tick for some weeks, an' 'e's got quite a bill. But Aw feels sorry for 'im' 'is wife really lams 'im at 'ome, an' Aw figure 'e needs t' get it off 'is chest — So 'e comes in, an' Aw says: "Tom — you owe me over two quid, now; when's it comin'?" "Gaw, Bianca," 'e says, "Aw just been out o' Collar, an' — "

DESDEMONA.   — "Out of Collar?"

BIANCA.   Wot yew call un-deployed ...

"Bianca," 'e says, "Gawd luv yew, me owld woman an' Aw've had a row an' Aw'm all done in. Aw'll pay th' soddin' bill, some'ow; but fer now, fer owld times," 'e says — well Gawd's Wounds, wot was Aw t'do? "Right, then, Tom," Aw said, an' Aw lays down on the bed — 'cause 'e liked me to go first — an' 'e puts the straps on me — "Tom," Aw says, "listen, luv, th' straps are bleedin' tight — " An' before Aw knew wot, 'e was lammin' me fer real!! 'E did me fer a jacketin' such as Aw thought would be me last L 'n' B!! Aw bite me teeth not to scream, 'cause the bobbies won't put up with no row, no matter how many quid Aw pay 'em.... Well, Tom finally gets it over wif, an' it's *my* turn. "Aw'm sorry, Bianca," 'e says, "if Aw got a bit rough." "Oh, it's nofin', Tom," Aw says — 'cause Aw'm determined t' get me own back.... So Aw tie 'im down on th' bed — 'e's a big strapper o' a bloke — An' then Aw lam th' *pudding* out o' 'im — !! An' 'e's 'ollerin' like it's th' Second Coming. Then after Aw gi 'im a royal pasting, Aw go through 'is togs, an' in the back pocket — Aw find a soddin' crown! "You been 'olding out on me, Tom! Aw've had it wi' yer dodges an' flams — wot kind o' a soup kitchen do yew fink me?" — An' Aw let into 'im again!! — "Bianca — let me go, an' Aw'll niver flam to ye again!" "BLEEDIN'-RIGHT!" Aw says. So Aw copped 'is brass, takes up the belt, an' let 'im loose — straight into the street 'e runs, naked as a blue-jay — Aw had to throw 'is togs after 'im. "Yew Owld Stringer!" Aw yelled: — "'Ere's yer togs, an' fer yer change, take this!" *(Bianca raises her fist and slaps her elbow; excited, she catches her breath.)*

DESDEMONA.   Jesus. Weren't you scared?

BIANCA.   Aw'd be lyin' if Aw said nay. Aw though it was me last trick. You can't be too careful, there's a lot of maggot-brained doodles in me bus'ness. But Aw can take care o' meself.

DESDEMONA.   Doesn't — doesn't it hurt?

BIANCA.   Naw — not usual. It's stingy-like, but it's all fakement. *(Bianca, looking into Desdemona's eyes, gets an idea.)* ... Aw c'n show you if you likes.... C'mon, it won't hurt you none —

DESDEMONA.   Well ... yes, all right, Bianca, show me.

Scene 22

The beating scene. Emilia, Bianca and Desdemona.

EMILIA.   Are you out o' your mind? Lettin' a strumpet strap you in your own house like a monk in Holy Week?

DESDEMONA.   Turn around, Emilia, and mind your own business. Go on, turn around, and say your beads. Pay no attention. *(To Bianca.)* Sorry — please continue. *(Emilia says her beads through the following.)*

EMILIA.   Hail Mary Full of Grace the Lord is with Thee —

BIANCA.   Get up on the table wi' yer tale end up —

EMILIA.   Holy Mary, Mother of — *(Emilia turns and sees Desdemona spread-eagled.)* — GOD!!!

BIANCA.   Right now. Aw'll just take a strap 'ere — an' Aw'll just brush you wi' it — but when Aw let's go, you move yer tail up — all right?

DESDEMONA.   I — I think so; it's rather like rising to the trot on a horse —

BIANCA.   Right then. One – up, Two – down; all right, now,
One: *(Desdemona moves up.)* Two – :   *(Bianca lightly straps
Desdemona as she moves down.)* One – :   *(Desdemona moves up.)*
An' Two – :   *(Desdemona moves down; a strap.)* — Does it hurt?

DESDEMONA.   No — no, it doesn't, really.

BIANCA.   Right then. Let's have some sound e-ffecks. One;
Two — *(Desdemona screams, Emilia clutches her rosary.)* — NO!!
— not that loud! The bobbies would be in on yew so fast yew
wouldn't get yer panties up — just a moan enow to get 'im
excited.... Right, then? Now: One – Two; One – Two; One –
Two; One – Two; One – Two; One – Two!! *(Desdemona perfects
her synchronized moans, building to a crescendo, at which point she
breaks into peals of laughter.)*

DESDEMONA.   It's smashing! — Mealy — you really must
try it!

Scene 23

As before.

BIANCA.   Aw want you t'take this in th' right way, now; but
if you weren't born a lady, you'd a been a bleedin'-good
blowzabella. One o' the best. An' — well, no matter what fate
holds, there's always room fer you in me shop. *(Bashful.)* Aw
means it, too —

EMILIA.   — Holy Mother, if anyone had so much as whis-
pered in Venice that you'd be makin' a bonnie whore, there'd
be a blood duel to settle in the streets!

BIANCA.   Aw'm payin' yer lady me respecks as one pro-
fessional t'anofer. You — you got as much notion of me craft
as a donkey has of Sunday.

EMILIA.   Why, thank you — at least someone has noted me
merit.

DESDEMONA.   *(Gently.)* I'm very complimented, Bianca ...
and I really did enjoy Tuesday night — but I don't think I'd

better risk covering for you again.

BIANCA.   — You're — you're not brimmin' fer me any-more?

DESDEMONA.   No — I don't think I'd better.

EMILIA.   *(To herself.)* Heigh-ho! On to the next —

BIANCA.   *(Trembling.)* But — but we c'n still be mates, wot?

DESDEMONA.   Of course we can! I want that very much. I never tire of hearing your stories. They're so lively, so very funny. What else have I got for amusement's sake. *(Bianca is disturbed. Emilia smiles.)* — but you haven't told me yet about your evening off with Cassio last Tuesday ... did you enjoy yourself?

BIANCA.   You don't want to 'ear about it none, it's not anyfing amusing —

DESDEMONA.   Now, just tell me all about it, Bianca; you can tell me your secrets, too. Woman to woman. What did you two do?

BIANCA.   *(Shy.)* We just talked.

EMILIA.   *(Snorting.)* *All* night?

BIANCA.   Yes! 'E's differnt, you know. 'E's a gen'l'man, 'e is — an' 'e makes the rest o' the blokes round 'ere look like the ninny-hammers they are —

EMILIA.   Oh, he's diff'rent, all right. You'd think after all week of tom-foolin' with the like of hicks, you'd have more sense than to go prancin' about with some *nancy* town stal-lion.

BIANCA.   Wot! Nancy! Nancy, is it? Who're you callin' "Nancy?"

DESDEMONA.   Now, Mealy, don't tease her —

EMILIA.   — the way I see it, it's no acc-i-dent for himself to be an army man —

BIANCA.   — Aw tell you wot, M'lord Cassio 'twill make a smug more obligin' in bed than the one you've got —

DESDEMONA.   *(Warningly.)* — Ladies, ladies —

EMILIA.   — Well, you'll never find out what it is to be havin' the like of a proper husband in the bed.

BIANCA.   Mayhap Aw will, too. Aw'm ready to let my way of life go fer wash the second 'e arsks me.

DESDEMONA. What!

BIANCA. Aw'm giving 'alfe me brass each week to the priest, Father Donahue, so's 'e c'n pray fer me sins an' t'gi' me apsolution — Aw'm ready t' say yes whenever 'e arsks me 'and — an' Aw c'n go to th' altar as unstained as you were on yer weddin' night.

EMILIA. *(Seeing Bianca in a new light.)* So — you're after goin' to the priest reg-ular? *(Impressed.)* That's a lot of money.

BIANCA. Bleedin'-right.

DESDEMONA. *(Crest-fallen.)* Oh, Bianca — oh, surely you're — you're not the type that wants to get married? *(Depressed, Desdemona goes and pours herself another mug of wine.)*

BIANCA. Wot's wrong wif that? Aw'm still young, an' Aw've got a tidy sum all saved up fer a dowry. An' m'lord Cassio's only got t'arsk fer a transfer to th' garrison 'ere; we'd make a bleedin'-jolly life of it, Aw c'n tell you. Aw'd get us a cottage by th' sea, wif winder-boxes an' all them kinds of fings, an' 'e could go to th' tipple'ouse as much as 'e likes, wifout me sayin' nay. An' then — then Aw'd be bearin' 'im sons so's to make 'im proud —

EMILIA. *(Triumphantly.)* There! There's your new woman, m'lady! Free! Does for herself!

BIANCA. Why, that "new woman" kind o' fing's all hogwash! *(Emilia nods her head in agreement.)* All women want t'get a smug, it's wot we're made for, ain't it? We may pretend differnt, but inside very born one o' us want smugs an' babies, smugs wot are man enow t' keep us in our place.

DESDEMONA. *(Quietly into her wine.)* I don't think I can stand it ...

BIANCA. 'Scusin' my cheek, but you're a lucky lady, an' you don't even know it. Your 'ubby might be wot you call a bit doo-lolly-tap-tap up 'ere — *(Bianca taps her head.)* — but th' maritle knot's tied good 'n' strong. Every time Aw 'ear — *(Dreamily.)* "'Til deaf do us part" — Aw starts t' snurfle. Aw can't 'elp it. If only Cassio would say them words an' make me th' 'appiest o' —

EMILIA. — And what makes you think m'lord Cassio — who's Venetian born, an' wears silk next to his skin, not none

38

of your Cyprus scum, is goin' to be marryin' a tried-on strumpet?

BIANCA.   'Coz a gen'l'men don't lie to a bird — Aw should soddin'-well know where ofs Aw speak. Besides, m'lord Cassio gi' me a "token o' 'is es-teem" —

EMILIA.   Hmmpf! And I'm after supposin' you gave him the same, as you've given tokens of esteem to all your customers — a scurvy clap — that's your token. *(Desdemona becomes curious.)*

DESDEMONA.   — Hush, Mealy. *(To Bianca.)* Never mind her, Bianca — I believe you. What type of token did Cassio give?

BIANCA.   *(As enthused as a teenage girl.)* It's a real flashy bit o' goods. It's a muckenger so swank Aw don't dare blow me beak in it. *(Confidentially.)* So Aw carry it down in me knockers an' next to me 'eart.

DESDEMONA.   *(Lost.)* — A swank ... muck ...

BIANCA.   — Wot Aw mean is, it ain't yer typic sneezer. *(Bianca gropes into her bodice, and tenderly takes out an embroidered handkerchief; proudly.)* 'Ere it is, now.

DESDEMONA.   *(Starting.)* — Why — *(Desdemona looks carefully, then in relief.)* Oh, thank God, Bianca, you've found it. I'm saved. *(Desdemona stops.)* But what — whatever are you doing with my handkerchief?

EMILIA.   *(To herself.)* Oh, Jesus, he gave it to Cassio!

BIANCA.   *(Blank.)* *Your* handkerchief? *Yours?!* *(Dangerously.)* What's Cassio doin' wi' your hand-ker-chief?

DESDEMONA.   That's precisely what I want to find out — Emilia —

BIANCA.   *(Fierce.)* — Aw bet. So — you was goin' t' 'elp me out once a week fer Cassio? *(Advancing.)* You cheatin' hussy — Aw'll pop yer peepers out — *(Bianca lunges for Desdemona; Emilia runs.)*

EMILIA.   — She's got a knife! —

DESDEMONA.   — Listen, Bianca —

BIANCA.   When Aw'm gulled by a woman, she don't live to do it twice —

DESDEMONA.   — Bianca, I swear! — *(Bianca sees the hoof-*

pick and picks it up, slowly advancing on Desdemona who clutches backs away towards the clothesline.)

BIANCA.   — Aw'll carve you up into cag-meat an' feed you to the pigs — Aw'll gag yer puddings out yer gob, you'll choke so hard —

DESDEMONA.   — I never! — *(Bianca swipes at Desdemona with the pick; the two clench each other; breaking away, Desdemona falls, and picks up a wine bottle in defense.)*

BIANCA.   Yer gonna snuff it, m'lady — so say yer prayers, yew goggle-eyed scab o' a WHORE ['ORE]. *(Desdemona ducks behind the hanging clothes, with Bianca following. We hear a scuffle, grunts and screams. Emilia runs for the palace door, calling.)*

EMILIA.   — GUARD! — GUARD — !! *(Emilia flings the door open. Then she realizes she can't call the guard, and quickly closes the door behind her, turning to face the room with grim desperation. Softly.)* Jesus.

BIANCA.   *(Off.)* — BLOODY! —

DESDEMONA.   *(Off.)* — MEALY!! *(Emilia runs away from the door, taking out her crucifix.)*

EMILIA.   Oh, Jesus. Oh, Jesus. *(And then, we hear a scream, a splash — and the sound of a bottle breaking. Slowly a dark, wet stain spreads on a cloth drying on the clothes-line. For a moment, there is silence. Bianca, looking grim and fierce, strides out from behind the clothes, holding the hoof-pick. She looks at Emilia, who backs away. There is a pause. Then, Desdemona steps from behind the hanging clothes, holding a broken wine bottle. The torso of her gown is splashed with dark, indelible burgundy. Softly.)* O, thank Jesus —

DESDEMONA.   Bianca!... Bianca, I never did.

BIANCA.   Leave me alone.... Aw've lost me chance of a smug! *(Bianca erupts into weeping, starts to wipe her nose with the handkerchief.)* — There! Take yer filthy linen! Aw wouldn't blow me nose in it —

DESDEMONA.   Bianca — I never did. I never did.

BIANCA.   Aw loved 'im —

DESDEMONA.   — Bianca —

BIANCA.   — An' Aw lost 'im —

DESDEMONA.   — Bianca —

BIANCA. — An' oh, oh, the cottage by the sea ...
DESDEMONA. If it makes a difference, I didn't.
BIANCA. — You gulled yer 'usband an' you gulled me!
An' Aw thought we was mates! *(Bianca starts to leave; Emilia calls after her.)*
EMILIA. I told you there's no such thing as friendship with ladies —
BIANCA. — You!! Washerdonna!! Shut yer potato-trap!
Don't you be so 'igh an' mighty smart!! *(Reaching the door, Bianca opens it, and turns.)* And just where was your Iago last Tuesday night! *(Triumphantly, Bianca slams the door behind her. A very long pause. Then, Desdemona tries to sound casual.)*
DESDEMONA. Um, Emilia, dear, just — just where was Iago last Tuesday night?
EMILIA. *(Distressed.)* He ... he said ... he said he was on guard duty ... *(Emilia begins to cry. Desdemona sits beside her, and tentatively puts her arms about Emilia. Then, Desdemona rocks her maid.)*

Scene 24

Lights up on Desdemona and Emilia, seated at the table, drinking wine, saying nothing.

Scene 25

Desdemona and Emilia, at table, staring ahead into air. Desdemona wearily looks into her cup, and pours herself and Emilia another cup of wine. They look at each other, nod to each other, and drink together.

Scene 26

Desdemona is drinking. Emilia grasps her own mug. Then, in a low voice.

EMILIA.   Do you know which one he was?
DESDEMONA.   No.... I don't think so. There were so many that night.
EMILIA.   Aye, you were having a proper time at it. Travellin' around the world!! *(Pause.)*
DESDEMONA.   There was one man ... *(Hesitating.)* It might have been him.
EMILIA.   *(Laughs harshly.)* My husband's a lover of garlic. Was that the man you're remembering?
DESDEMONA.   No — it's not that — although ...
EMILIA.   Well, what is it you remember!
DESDEMONA.   There was one man who ... didn't last very long.
EMILIA.   Aye. That's the one.

Scene 27

The same.

EMILIA.   When I was married in the Church, the knot tied beneath the Virgin's nose, I looked forward to the bed with as much joy as any girl after a hard day. And then Iago — well, he was still a lad, with the softness of a boy, and who could tell he'd turn into the man? *(Emilia pauses to drink.)* But all that girl-nonsense was knocked out of me by the nights. Night followin' night, as sure as the day's work came after. I'd stretch myself out on the bed, you see, waitin' for my good man to come to me and be my mate — as the Priest said he could — but then. But then I saw it didn't matter what had gone on between us — the fights, my crying, a good meal or a cold one. Days could pass without a word between us —

and he'd take his fill of me the same. I could have been the bed itself. And so, you see, I vowed not to be there for him. As he'd be lying on me in the dark, I'd picture up my rosary, so real I could kiss the silver. And I'd start at the Blessed Cross itself, while he was somewhere doin' his business above, and I'd say the first wooden bead, and then I'd finger the next bead in my mind, and then onto the next — *(Emila stops.)* But I never did make it to the medallion. He'd be all through with me by the time of the third "Hail Mary." *(Pause.)* Does my lady know what I'm saying?

DESDEMONA.   I'm not sure. I ... I don't think it's ... happened to me like that.

EMILIA.   Ah, well, men are making fools of themselves over you. The Ambassador is traipsing from the mainland just to hold onto your skirt; and your husband — *(Emilia stops herself.)* — Well, maybe it's all different for the likes of you. *(Desdemona says nothing.)* And then, maybe not. It's hard to be seeing, when you're young and men watch you when you pass them by, and the talkin' stops between them. But all in all, in time you'll know. Women just don't figure in their heads — not the one who hangs the wash, not Bianca — and not even you, m'lady. That's the hard truth. Men only see each other in their eyes. Only each other. *(Beat.)* And that's why I'm ready to leave the whole pack of them behind and go with you and the Ambassador. Oh, to see my husband's face to-morrow morning! When he finds out that I can get along by myself, with no thanks to his plotting and hatching!   — But it's leave him now or be countin' my beads through the years, waitin' for his last breath!

DESDEMONA.   *(Quietly.)* Emilia — I'll be honest with you, even if it puts me in risk to do so.... You're to stay behind tomorrow. I've asked my cousin for my own safe passage. I wish to go alone with Ludovico. *(Emilia stands very still.)* I am in your hands. You can run and tell my husband all — but I don't want to trifle with your feelings and desert you with the first tide. This way, you see, I'm only temporarily leaving you behind. But I promise I'll need your service in Venice as much as tonight. So, you're to follow me when all household

43

matters are in hand, taking with you whatever my husband permits. As a token of my esteem — here — *(Desdemona takes off a ring, and gazes at it wistfully.)* I want you to have this. It's a momento given me by Ludovico for — well, never you mind what for. Little did he think it would wind up 'round the finger of an honest woman. *(Desdemona gives the ring to Emilia.)*

EMILIA.   This ring is for me? but it's of value, m'lady — *(Emilia tries to return it; Desdemona insists. Emilia makes a decision.)* Listen, Miss, you've gone and leveled with me, and I'm after doing the same with you — *(Emila blurts.)* — M'lady, don't go to your husband's bed tonight. Lie apart — stay in my chamber.

DESDEMONA.   Why? Whatever for? It would raise suspicion.

EMILIA.   I'll say you're ill — with woman sickness.

DESDEMONA.   But why?

EMILIA.   Because ... because ... oh, m'lady, you know how easy it is to be seduced by a husband's soft word, when it's the like of angry words he pours down upon your head —

DESDEMONA.   *(Very still.)* Emilia — what have you done?

EMILIA.   I took the handkerchief.

DESDEMONA.   You took the handkerchief.... I thought you did.

EMILIA.   It was to be a joke, you see; my husband put me up to it, as a lark, he said, just to see —

DESDEMONA.   *(Very softly.)* — Iago — Oh, my sweet Jesus —

EMILIA.   And he was laughing about it, ye see, and he was as gay as a boy; he said he'd just ... hide it for a while, all in jest —

DESDEMONA.   Oh, no — he ... he must have ... planted it on Cassio — that's why ...

EMILIA.   It was just for a lark!

DESDEMONA.   Emilia — what has your husband been thinking!

EMILIA.   I don't know what he thinks. *(Desdemona twists the handkerchief.)*

DESDEMONA.   What use is this to me now! If I return it,

44

my husband will say that my lover gave it back to me!!

EMILIA. Miss Desdemona — oh my lady, I'm sure your husband loves you!

DESDEMONA. How do you know that my husband — !

EMILIA. — More than the world! He won't harm you none, m'lady — I've often seen him —

DESDEMONA. — What have you seen?!

EMILIA. I've seen him, sometimes when you walk in the garden, slip behind the arbor just to watch you, unawares ... and at night ... in the corridor ... outside your room — sometimes he just stands there, Miss, when you're asleep — he just stands there —

DESDEMONA. *(Frightened.)* Oh, Jesus —

EMILIA. And once ... I saw ... I came upon him unbeknowin', and he didn't see me, I'm sure — he was in your chamber room — and he gathered up the sheets from your bed, like a body, and ... and he held it to his face, like, like a bouquet, all breathin' it in — *(The two women pause: they both realize Othello's been smelling the sheets for traces of a lover.)*

DESDEMONA. That isn't love. It isn't love. *(Beat.)* Why didn't you tell me this before?

EMILIA. *(Carefully.)* I always thought it was not my place. *(The two women do not speak for a moment. Emilia looks towards the palace door.)* Well, what are we to be doin' now?

DESDEMONA. We have to make it to the morning. You'd better come with me — it's not safe for you, either. *(Emilia says nothing.)* We'll have to leave all behind. It's not safe to pack. *(Desdemona thinks, carefully.)* Now listen, carefully, Emilia. I'll go to my own chamber tonight. You're to wait up for my husband's return — tell him I'm ill and I've taken to my own bed. He's not to disturb me, I'm not well. I'll turn in before he comes, and I'll ... pretend to sleep if he should come to me. *(Pause.)* Surely he'll not ... harm a sleeping woman.

EMILIA. I'll do it.

DESDEMONA. Good. I'd better go to bed. *(Desdemona starts towards the palace door and stops.)*

EMILIA.   Would you like me to brush your hair tonight? A hundred strokes?
DESDEMONA.   Oh, yes, please, Emilia ...

Scene 28

Emilia brushes Desdemona's hair. Desdemona leans back, tense, listening to the off-stage palace.

EMILIA.   Now, then — *(Emilia starts.)* One, two, three, four, five, six —

Scene 29

The same.

EMILIA.   Forty-five, forty-six, forty-seven —

Scene 30

Desdemona and Emilia. Emilia reaches the hundredth stroke.

EMILIA.   Ninety-seven ... ninety-eight ... ninety-nine ... *(They freeze. Blackout.)*

END OF PLAY

PROPERTY PLOT

ON STAGE

Square, metal washtub with:
    large rock
    bloody sheet
    water
Round washtub with:
    linens
Stool
Terrycloth towel
Antique towel
Wooden crate with:
    patterned skirt
    cream-colored robe
    white bloomers
    white fancy nightshirt
Clothes line
Curtain set
2 metal buckets with chain
Velcro sheet
Lace camisole
Grey sweat pants
Wine-stained gown
Barrels
Throne with:
    robe on right side
    fan on seat
Glass with wine
Broken bottle
Basket with:
    clothes pins attached in bag
    plain sheet
    semi-flannel sheet
    grey sweat pants

Shelf with:
  - leather strap
  - hoof pick
  - white lace camisole
  - basket with lid
  - broom
  - Ludovico's note
  - Desdemona's slippers

Basket with burlap
Short bucket with cloth
Crate with wine bottles
Bucket of clean water
Sack of potatoes
Colander
Paring knife
Basket with handles with:
  - pink pillow case
  - 2 white pillow cases with buttons
  - drawstring shorts
  - handkerchief
  - camisole

Crate with:
  - mask
  - bowl of soup
  - spoon
  - pita

Basket with:
  - sewing kit
  - grey sweat pants
  - lace-up camisole
  - crotchless shorts, with threaded needle ready to sew
  - brown knickers, with threaded needle ready to sew
  - white embroidered dressing gown, with needle ready to sew

Brass basin with:
  - water
  - pumice stone
  - cuticle stick
  - wash cloth

OFF STAGE

Wine bottle (half full with tea)
2 goblets

PERSONAL

Note from Ludovico (EMILIA)
Handkerchief (DESDEMONA)
Strawberry handkerchief (BIANCA)
Coins (BIANCA)

COSTUME PLOT

Emilia

2 striped cotton headwraps
1 gray textured cotton apron
1 green wool gauze peasant blouse
1 muslin petticoat
1 black and beige tweed raw silk jumper
1 pair black flats
1 beige lightly padded bra

Bianca

1 wine and red silk open jumper
1 wine Fortuny pleated underskirt
1 short sleeve white and gold lycra top, distressed
1 pair Etienne Aigner tan leather sandals
1 ikat design cotton batiste headwrap (wines, reds, fuschias)

Desdemona

1 white silk charmeuse chemise, 8" lace at hem
   (white brocade empire corset attached)
2 white silk jacquard robes, one wine stained
1 gold lame brocade hooded robe
1 pair American Eagle pink crochet slippers
1 pair white silk charmeuse tap pants

Accessories

Emilia

1 leather necklace with cross
1 beige seed rosary
1 muslin handkerchief

Bianca

1 1" black elastic garter
1 pair silver hoop earrings with red drops
1 leather thong necklace with silver and red ceramic beads
1 wine braid choker
1 multi-colored Venetian glass bead anklet
1 small beaded twisted bracelet, red, white, and black
1 string small glass beads, red, blue, green (necklace used as a bracelet)
1 silver and gold ball-link belt
1 Chinese embroidered money bag

Desdemona

1 silver ring with moon stone
1 gold wedding band
1 pair gold, diamond, and pearl earrings

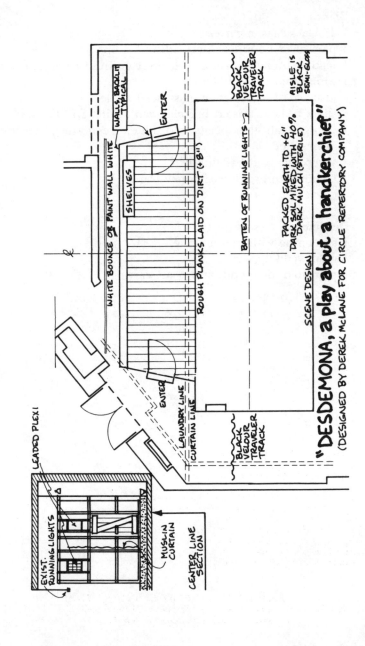

"DESDEMONA, a play about a handkerchief"

(DESIGNED BY DEREK McLANE FOR CIRCLE REPERTORY COMPANY)

NEW PLAYS

★ **BE AGGRESSIVE by Annie Weisman.** Vista Del Sol is paradise, sandy beaches, avocado-lined streets. But for seventeen-year-old cheerleader Laura, everything changes when her mother is killed in a car crash, and she embarks on a journey to the Spirit Institute of the South where she can learn "cheer" with Bible belt intensity. "…filled with lingual gymnastics…stylized rapid-fire dialogue…" –*Variety*. "…a new, exciting, and unique voice in the American theatre…" –*BackStage West*. [1M, 4W, extras] ISBN: 0-8222-1894-1

★ **FOUR by Christopher Shinn.** Four people struggle desperately to connect in this quiet, sophisticated, moving drama. "…smart, broken-hearted…Mr. Shinn has a precocious and forgiving sense of how power shifts in the game of sexual pursuit…He promises to be a playwright to reckon with…" –*NY Times*. "A voice emerges from an American place. It's got humor, sadness and a fresh and touching rhythm that tell of the loneliness and secrets of life…[a] poetic, haunting play." –*NY Post*. [3M, 1W] ISBN: 0-8222-1850-X

★ **WONDER OF THE WORLD by David Lindsay-Abaire.** A madcap picaresque involving Niagara Falls, a lonely tour-boat captain, a pair of bickering private detectives and a husband's dirty little secret. "Exceedingly whimsical and playfully wicked. Winning and genial. A top-drawer production." –*NY Times*. "Full frontal lunacy is on display. A most assuredly fresh and hilarious tragicomedy of marital discord run amok…absolutely hysterical…" –*Variety*. [3M, 4W (doubling)] ISBN: 0-8222-1863-1

★ **QED by Peter Parnell.** Nobel Prize-winning physicist and all-around genius Richard Feynman holds forth with captivating wit and wisdom in this fascinating biographical play that originally starred Alan Alda. "QED is a seductive mix of science, human affections, moral courage, and comic eccentricity. It reflects on, among other things, death, the absence of God, travel to an unexplored country, the pleasures of drumming, and the need to know and understand." –*NY Magazine*. "Its rhythms correspond to the way that people—even geniuses—approach and avoid highly emotional issues, and it portrays Feynman with affection and awe." –*The New Yorker*. [1M, 1W] ISBN: 0-8222-1924-7

★ **UNWRAP YOUR CANDY by Doug Wright.** Alternately chilling and hilarious, this deliciously macabre collection of four bedtime tales for adults is guaranteed to keep you awake for nights on end. "Engaging and intellectually satisfying…a treat to watch." –*NY Times*. "Fiendishly clever. Mordantly funny and chilling. Doug Wright teases, freezes and zaps us." –*Village Voice*. "Four bite-size plays that bite back." –*Variety*. [flexible casting] ISBN: 0-8222-1871-2

★ **FURTHER THAN THE FURTHEST THING by Zinnie Harris.** On a remote island in the middle of the Atlantic secrets are buried. When the outside world comes calling, the islanders find their world blown apart from the inside as well as beyond. "Harris winningly produces an intimate and poetic, as well as political, family saga." –*Independent (London)*. "Harris' enthralling adventure of a play marks a departure from stale, well-furrowed theatrical terrain." –*Evening Standard (London)*. [3M, 2W] ISBN: 0-8222-1874-7

★ **THE DESIGNATED MOURNER by Wallace Shawn.** The story of three people living in a country where what sort of books people like to read and how they choose to amuse themselves becomes both firmly personal and unexpectedly entangled with questions of survival. "This is a playwright who does not just tell you what it is like to be arrested at night by goons or to fall morally apart and become an aimless yet weirdly contented ghost yourself. He has the originality to make you feel it." –*Times (London)*. "A fascinating play with beautiful passages of writing…" –*Variety*. [2M, 1W] ISBN: 0-8222-1848-8

DRAMATISTS PLAY SERVICE, INC.
440 Park Avenue South, New York, NY 10016   212-683-8960   Fax 212-213-1539
postmaster@dramatists.com   www.dramatists.com

NEW PLAYS

★ SHEL'S SHORTS by Shel Silverstein. Lauded poet, songwriter and author of children's books, the incomparable Shel Silverstein's short plays are deeply infused with the same wicked sense of humor that made him famous. "...[a] childlike honesty and twisted sense of humor." *—Boston Herald.* "...terse dialogue and an absurdity laced with a tang of dread give [*Shel's Shorts*] more than a trace of Samuel Beckett's comic existentialism." *—Boston Phoenix.* [flexible casting] ISBN: 0-8222-1897-6

★ AN ADULT EVENING OF SHEL SILVERSTEIN by Shel Silverstein. Welcome to the darkly comic world of Shel Silverstein, a world where nothing is as it seems and where the most innocent conversation can turn menacing in an instant. These ten imaginative plays vary widely in content, but the style is unmistakable. "...[*An Adult Evening*] shows off Silverstein's virtuosic gift for wordplay...[and] sends the audience out...with a clear appreciation of human nature as perverse and laughable." *—NY Times.* [flexible casting] ISBN: 0-8222-1873-9

★ WHERE'S MY MONEY? by John Patrick Shanley. A caustic and sardonic vivisection of the institution of marriage, laced with the author's inimitable razor-sharp wit. "...Shanley's gift for acid-laced one-liners and emotionally tumescent exchanges is certainly potent..." *—Variety.* "...lively, smart, occasionally scary and rich in reverse wisdom." *—NY Times.* [3M, 3W] ISBN: 0-8222-1865-8

★ A FEW STOUT INDIVIDUALS by John Guare. A wonderfully screwy comedy-drama that figures Ulysses S. Grant in the throes of writing his memoirs, surrounded by a cast of fantastical characters, including the Emperor and Empress of Japan, the opera star Adelina Patti and Mark Twain. "Guare's smarts, passion and creativity skyrocket to awesome heights..." *—Star Ledger.* "...precisely the kind of good new play that you might call an everyday miracle...every minute of it is fresh and newly alive..." *—Village Voice.* [10M, 3W] ISBN: 0-8222-1907-7

★ BREATH, BOOM by Kia Corthron. A look at fourteen years in the life of Prix, a Bronx native, from her ruthless girl-gang leadership at sixteen through her coming to maturity at thirty. "...vivid world, believable and eye-opening, a place worthy of a dramatic visit, where no one would want to live but many have to." *—NY Times.* "...rich with humor, terse vernacular strength and gritty detail..." *—Variety.* [1M, 9W] ISBN: 0-8222-1849-6

★ THE LATE HENRY MOSS by Sam Shepard. Two antagonistic brothers, Ray and Earl, are brought together after their father, Henry Moss, is found dead in his seedy New Mexico home in this classic Shepard tale. "...His singular gift has been for building mysteries out of the ordinary ingredients of American family life..." *—NY Times.* "...rich moments ...Shepard finds gold." *—LA Times.* [7M, 1W] ISBN: 0-8222-1858-5

★ THE CARPETBAGGER'S CHILDREN by Horton Foote. One family's history spanning from the Civil War to WWII is recounted by three sisters in evocative, intertwining monologues. "...bittersweet music—[a] rhapsody of ambivalence...in its modest, garrulous way...theatrically daring." *—The New Yorker.* [3W] ISBN: 0-8222-1843-7

★ THE NINA VARIATIONS by Steven Dietz. In this funny, fierce and heartbreaking homage to *The Seagull*, Dietz puts Chekhov's star-crossed lovers in a room and doesn't let them out. "A perfect little jewel of a play..." *—Shepherdstown Chronicle.* "...a delightful revelation of a writer at play; and also an odd, haunting, moving theater piece of lingering beauty." *—Eastside Journal (Seattle).* [1M, 1W (flexible casting)] ISBN: 0-8222-1891-7

DRAMATISTS PLAY SERVICE, INC.
440 Park Avenue South, New York, NY 10016 212-683-8960 Fax 212-213-1539
postmaster@dramatists.com   www.dramatists.com